The SURVIVING DEPRESSION
Journal

A Catholic Approach

Kathryn James Hermes, FSP
with Mary Elizabeth Tebo, FSP

Pauline
BOOKS & MEDIA

Boston

Library of Congress Cataloging-in-Publication Data

Hermes, Kathryn.
Surviving depression journal : a Catholic approach / Kathryn James Hermes.
  p. cm.
ISBN 0-8198-7104-4 (pbk.)
1. Depressed persons—Religious life. 2. Depression, Mental—Religious aspects—Catholic
Church. I. Title.
BV4910.34.H475 2007
248.8'625—dc22

                          2007022125

Cover design by Rosana Usselmann

Interior photos: Mary Emmanuel Alves, FSP

Interior graphic: istockphoto.com

Published by Pauline Books & Media, 50 Saint Paul's Avenue, Boston, MA 02130-3491.
www.pauline.org.

Printed in the U.S.A.

Pauline Books & Media is the publishing house of the Daughters of St. Paul, an international congregation of women religious serving the Church with the communications media.

1 2 3 4 5 6 7 8 9   12 11 10 09 08

Contents

Introduction

If you picked up this book, you have not done so by mistake. It is a sign of God's love for you, of God's desire to seek you out, even on the frustrating and soul-searing journey of depression. God put it in your path.

Before moving ahead, I invite you to say the following words to yourself to prepare you for what's ahead:

God, I want a companion in my struggle, and I want to survive this depression. You are leading me, yet I have a hard time finding your hand and holding on tight. Guide me step by step in your path that I may glorify you and be filled with the radiance of one who has trusted and discovered how trustworthy you are. Give me the strength not to shrink before the path of prayer and communion with you, which will be one of the most profound "therapies" I will take in my journey to wholeness. I trust you. Amen.

In *Surviving Depression: A Catholic Approach*, *Prayers for Surviving Depression*, and *The Journal for Surviving Depression* you will find a fresh way of approaching the struggle to surviving depression rooted in the spiritual and sacramental life of the Catholic Church.

This book is offered as a companion to anyone attempting to navigate the confusing labyrinth of a mood disorder. It arises out of my own experience. In 1985, when I was in my early twenties, I had a stroke during outpatient surgery. It was the beginning of the rest of my life. I have since suffered serious bouts of depression as well as TLE (temporal lobe epilepsy), an organic bipolar disorder.

Depression—often accompanied by confused thinking, mood swings, isolation, or despair—makes life feel rotten. Quicksand replaces solid ground and exhaustion replaces energy. When I have been spinning out of control, it has been trusted friends who have guided me back to calm. My hope is that this book can be one such friend to anyone looking for meaning, order, and hope in the midst of confusing, conflicting emotions. It can help in remaking essential connections to healthy thinking, and it guides the reader gently on the path of prayer and contemplation.

This journal can be used with the book *Surviving Depression: A Catholic Approach* or on its own. The structured material is balanced by empty space for the artist, doodler, or non-linear person.

However you choose to use this book, remember one thing: each step of the way, you will be invited to open your heart just a little bit more to the possibilities of desire—the desires buried beneath the depression in your own heart, and the desires God has for you working in and through your struggle with depression. You are bigger than the depression. Cynicism may seem safer, anger may seem easier, but the journey of contemplation will reap you the most abundant and satisfying rewards!

CHAPTER 1

What Does Depression Look Like?

Spiritual Directions

The line was long, stretching into the next room. People suffering from depression wanted a word of hope, a miracle, something that would change the darkness to light.... Tired, I gave my attention to the gentleman before me. "You see, my depression doesn't seem to go away. I always feel down. It's hard to keep a job. I don't want to do anything. Nothing seems to help. My wife doesn't know what to do with me anymore. I just wish I could feel happy again."

As you begin this journal, what is it you desire?

Copy this phrase below: *I am held safe. I am loved. I am protected.*

_____

_____

_____

_____

Moment of Contemplation

Remember a time in your life when you felt loved by a friend or parent, a time when you were astounded by the love shown to another, or a time when you felt moved by the goodness shown to you by a stranger. Allow that moment of love to penetrate all the layers of your being so that you feel moved once more by the experience.

Sit quietly. Rest. Wait. Journal your thoughts, feelings, desires.

Holy Darkness

Evelyn Underhill, born in England in 1875, was a remarkable spiritual writer and guide. Her letters of spiritual direction, full of practical wisdom, firmly yet gently led people to embrace their reality. For those who suffer with depression, the present moment can be painfully dark and exhausting. We wonder if we can have any spiritual life at all, because there are no radiant experiences or ecstatic prayer. These words from Underhill can be a relief:

> You will have just common grey weather and storm and fog and perhaps even intense darkness before you have done—that's all part of the "Leave all and follow Me." But it's all right. I would not forecast anything or try to look ahead or wonder how much you can bear—just leave yourselves in God's Hand. "I am with thee, saith the Lord."[1]

What would you like to say to God?

_____

_____

_____

_____

_____

_____

_____

_____

_____

Personal Pages Between God and You

"You who are weary and sad and heavy burdened,
come to me, come yet again,
come and it will make me so happy to be able to refresh you."

(cf. Mt 11:28)

This is what God wants: a relationship with you. Depression can seem to block you from this relationship. Often people feel cheated, put aside, or forgotten by God when they are depressed. Sometimes we can blame God for causing the events or illness that have brought on our depression. God is a safe person to blame. After all, he seems so distant when one is suffering with depression. Nevertheless, God is never far away, and he always desires a relationship with you. God continuously breathes life into you, keeping you in existence. God understands how hard it is for you.

How do you feel about your relationship with God?

If you can't feel any connection with God right now, what would be the sign that would convince you, beyond any shadow of a doubt, that you are loved by God? Can you find even a little bit of that "evidence" of God's love right now in your life?

What do you imagine would be the most wonderful thing God could want from you? For you?

doodles · hopes · fears · lights · prayers · mercies · words · dreams · tears · joys

joys · tears · dreams · words · mercies · prayers · lights · fears · hopes · doodles

doodles · hopes · fears · lights · prayers · mercies · words · dreams · tears · joys

joys · tears · dreams · words · mercies · prayers · lights · fears · hopes · doodles

comfort

Let God In

Take a moment and let God in. Invite him into the places of your heart and your life that you most want to hide from him. Ask him to speak to you about these places and to give you the courage to begin to trust him with your life in ever deeper ways.

Yes, Lord, please come. I invite you into my heart and into my life. I give you permission to walk through the rooms of my heart and the halls of my life. Visit with your healing presence. Come to me here. Come heal me here.

Sit quietly. Rest. Wait. Journal your thoughts, feelings, desires.

_____

_____

_____

_____

_____

_____

_____

_____

_____

_____

_____

_____

· mercies · words · dreams · tears · joys

· prayers · lights · fears · hopes · doodles

CHAPTER 2

"If Only You Tried Harder"

Spiritual Directions

For the umpteenth time, my friend stopped in my office and began to tell her story. It always began the same way. "It hurts so much. It's so dark. I don't think I can go on. Why does it have to be this way? Where is God?" I knew *her* story by heart, but barely remember the countless times *I* told my own story to a chosen friend, Karen, during my own long years of therapy while struggling with depression. Yet, Karen reminds me now and then, and is grateful that I remember that *she* was there for me when *I* most needed it. We need to tell our stories over and over again before we see the light.

Now, why don't you tell your story?

Copy this phrase below: *O God, come and save me now.*

_____

_____

_____

Moment of Contemplation

To worship God in the midst of adversity and misfortune is to understand fully who we are in relation to God. Imagine yourself before God, bowing low in adoration, perhaps unable to speak, or perhaps even angry at God. Allow yourself to worship and to praise despite your feelings. What is this experience like?

Sit quietly. Rest. Wait. Journal your thoughts, feelings, desires.

_____

_____

_____

_____

_____

_____

_____

_____

_____

_____

_____

_____

_____

_____

Holy Darkness

These words, by Chiara Lubich, religious leader and contemporary spiritual writer, have particular meaning for someone struggling to worship God in the midst of the chaos of depression:

> I love you
> not because I learned to tell you so,
> not because my heart suggests these words to me,
> not so much because faith
> makes me believe that you are love,
> not even for the sole reason that
> you died for me.
> I love you because you entered my life
> more than the air in my lungs,
> more than the blood in my veins.
> You entered
> where no one could enter,
> when no one could help me,
> every single time no one
> could console me.[2]

What would you like to say to God?

_____

_____

_____

_____

_____

_____

_____

Personal Pages Between God and You

I am close to the broken hearted.
Those who are crushed in spirit I shall save.

(cf. Ps 34:18)

It isn't easy to believe that God loves you when you feel so awful, when everything in you seems shrouded in darkness and fear, when you run from every haunting memory that surfaces on the waves of your consciousness. But remembering the truth that God is close to you is the one memory that will root you in reality.

What do you desire God to do for you?

What are the memories that frighten you?

Is there one memory of someone who has loved you?

What did it feel like to be loved?

Can you allow yourself to believe that God loves you at least as much as this person loves you?

doodles · hopes · fears · lights · prayers · mercies · words · dreams · tears · joys

joys · tears · dreams · words · mercies · prayers · lights · fears · hopes · doodles

doodles · hopes · fears · lights · prayers · mercies · words · dreams · tears · joys

joys · tears · dreams · words · mercies · prayers · lights · fears · hopes · doodles

remember

Let God In

Take a moment and let God in. Invite him into the places of your heart and your life that you most want to hide from him. Ask him to speak to you about these places and to give you the courage to begin to trust him with your life in ever deeper ways.

Yes, Lord, please come. I invite you into my heart and into my life. I give you permission to walk through the rooms of my heart and the halls of my life. Visit with your healing presence. Come to me here. Come heal me here.

Sit quietly. Rest. Wait. Journal your thoughts, feelings, desires.

Letters from God

You want to know that someone really understands you, and so you tell your story again and again. You talk about emotional wounds, injustices, medicine, and therapy, hoping that in the telling something within you will settle. I hear your story. I was there when you were created. I cried when injustices were inflicted on you. I listen to your heart as you speak with your lips. I am here, right here in your heart. You don't have to tell me your story for me to know it—I already know your story entirely—but I still love to hear it from your own lips. Your telling your story to me is "divine therapy," because when you speak with me, I can speak with you. I never tire of listening to you even when you repeat yourself. At some point, in the midst of the telling, you will realize that you have found everything that you were looking for, and the story will take on a new quality. Then it will become a history of what you have received from me and from others, a recounting of the history of your salvation. Others will rejoice to hear this story, and they will find strength and hope in its details. So don't be afraid of repeating yourself when speaking with me. I love the sound of your voice, and I am eternally invested in every detail of your being and your life.

doodles · hopes · fears · lights · prayers · mercies · words · dreams · tears · joys

joys · tears · dreams · words · mercies · prayers · lights · fears · hopes · doodles

CHAPTER 3

"Why Doesn't God Heal Me?"

Spiritual Directions

I was sitting alone in our guest house for the third day, trying to relax. It had been a long year with an extraordinary load of work. Finally, after three days alone in the silence, I was beginning to feel like myself again. While typing out a list of symptoms for depression in a manuscript I was working on, I had realized that I was depressed. The tears I had shed the Monday before had not just been tears of weariness; they had been a sign of the depression I had been ignoring in order to accomplish the impossible. I realized I would have to ask for help to complete my work. I felt ashamed for once again not being able to measure up.

And you, what have been your losses and how painful has this been for you?

Copy this phrase below: *I am a good person, just as I am.*

_____

_____

Moment of Contemplation

Remember a time when someone treated you with respect. How did it make you feel? What words or actions did he or she use to express his or her respect? What was that like? Have you ever shown respect for someone else? What is it like to give respect to another?

Sit quietly. Rest. Wait. Journal your thoughts, feelings, desires.

_____

_____

_____

_____

_____

_____

_____

_____

_____

_____

_____

_____

_____

_____

_____

_____

Holy Darkness

Poets and theologians have used many images to express the wintering of the soul and the promise of spring. Few, however, equal George Herbert's (1593–1633) eloquent description, in his poem "The Flower," of the barren "lostness" of winter, the time in which flowers depart to "see their mother root." Flower and root, dead to the world, "keep house unknown" during the hard weather. It's in the spring, Herbert exclaims, almost with unbelieving ecstasy, that his heart, once shriveled in the winter cold, had refound its "greenness."[3] With similar imagery, a friend of mine shared with me a poem she wrote during a difficult time:

> How could my heart not have believed
> that the miracle of spring could not descend
> also on its barren landscape
> breaking open the buried seed
> pulsing with new life?[4]

In a sermon St. Augustine said that our winterness is the promise of the hiddenness of Christ. The winter seems to kill all that lives, even down to the root, but instead the root lives on.[5]

What would you like to say to God?

Personal Pages Between God and You

God has started doing marvelous things in you.
He won't stop, he will bring his masterpiece to completion
so that you are complete when Jesus Christ comes again.

(cf. Phil 1:6)

You are something beautiful that God is creating at every moment. God can hate nothing he has made. God's love for his creation is stronger than a mother's love, more faithful than a father's love, more enduring than the seasons, and more gentle than the softest rain coaxing new life from the earth. Depression can make us feel ugly, a failure, hopeless. Depression can trick us into thinking that because we *feel* hopeless we *are* hopeless. The only way out of this quicksand of feelings is to continually confront ourselves with ideas, images, and thoughts that tell us otherwise. Favorite books, movies, music, passages of Scripture, and friends can keep telling us the truth about God and ourselves until we can discover that what they are saying *is* true, until we can feel our own worth and beauty.

What are some signs of God's love for you? Can you count your blessings in the past day—even seemingly small blessings, such as a friend calling, or the sun pouring in your window, or waking up on time?

What is the most wonderful thing God has done for you? Read a favorite book or listen to a song that has special meaning for you. Write out the phrases and images that confront your feelings about yourself.

doodles · hopes · fears · lights · prayers · mercies · words · dreams · tears · joys

joys · tears · dreams · words · mercies · prayers · lights · fears · hopes · doodles

Let God In

Take a moment and let God in. Invite him into the places of your heart and your life that you most want to hide from him. Ask him to speak to you about these places and to give you the courage to begin to trust him with your life in ever deeper ways.

Yes, Lord, please come. I invite you into my heart and into my life. I give you permission to walk through the rooms of my heart and the halls of my life. Visit with your healing presence. Come to me here. Come heal me here.

Sit quietly. Rest. Wait. Journal your thoughts, feelings, desires.

_____

_____

_____

_____

_____

_____

_____

_____

_____

_____

_____

_____

Letters from God

It's hard for you to let go because so much is at stake. You want to be strong enough, stable enough, good enough to be assured of respect and security. I too am interested in your good name and I want you to be secure. My plans are for your good. You may need to relinquish the little security you think you have in order to discover the greater security I promise. I know how hard it is, and I am patient while you get up your courage.

doodles · hopes · fears · lights · prayers · mercies · words · dreams · tears · joys

joys · tears · dreams · words · mercies · prayers · lights · fears · hopes · doodles

CHAPTER 4

"How Do I Start?"

Spiritual Directions

One rainy night Jaleen, an alcoholic suffering with depression, was driving home when someone darted in front of her car. She slammed on the brakes as a teenager threw himself onto the sidewalk to avoid being hit. Jaleen got out of her car to check on the young man, shaking at how close she had come to hitting him. In seconds police surrounded them. Before Jaleen could say a word, they were handcuffing and leading the teenager away. "You don't understand," she said, "*I* almost hit *him*." An officer replied, "Mam, we saw the whole thing. He just robbed the corner store." Jaleen was dumbfounded. Later she recalled how something profound happened during the incident. "When I slammed on the breaks, I heard these words: 'I've made you for better things than this.' I knew it was time to get help."

When did you realize you needed to ask for help?

Copy this phrase below: *You, Lord, are my shepherd.*

_____

_____

Moment of Contemplation

When you began your first steps to well-being, was there anyone there to help you? What made it particularly difficult? What did you hope to achieve? What has been your journey?

Sit quietly. Rest. Wait. Journal your thoughts, feelings, desires.

In 1949, T. S. Eliot wrote the play, *The Cocktail Party*, for the Edinburgh Festival. This play presents desperately lonely characters. Each character is weak, superficial, and incoherent. Amidst all of these restless, petty souls we meet at the cocktail party, there is one great soul, Celia, who is unconscious of herself, who must be brought to life. She is of a different caliber than the other characters, and she feels restless and depressed by the arid atmosphere. One mysterious gentleman at the cocktail party, later revealed to be a psychiatrist, speaks with Celia and probes her spiritual condition and the deeper human desires motivating her to seek something beyond the superficial pleasantries surrounding her. He gives her two options: to accept a simple reconciliation to the human condition or to follow her inner vision. It is a way that is unknown and requires faith—"the kind of faith that issues from despair."

On the journey one knows very little, one is blind. To embark on this way demands a free and conscious decision with lasting repercussions. The way leads toward possession of what one had previously sought in the wrong place. Very slowly the springtime that the initiate "suffers" works a painful transformation.[6]

What would you like to say to God?

_____

_____

_____

_____

_____

_____

Personal Pages Between God and You

When Jesus saw a man who had been ill for thirty-eight years lying near the pool of Bethsaida, he said to him, "Do you want to be made well?"

(cf. Jn 5:6)

When God is going to do his deepest work in you, it will begin with this question, "Do you want to be made well?" And he will respect your response. This answer, this yes to the journey toward wellness, may be the hardest and the longest yes you will ever say in your life. What makes it hard is that in answering yes, you voluntarily surrender to an unknown future. You agree to leave behind control, security, and the cocoon we all spin around ourselves, protecting our dependence on the very things that are ruining our lives. It is the longest yes because it starts at the beginning and ends only at our death. It takes a lifetime to really become "well." But it is worth every second of the journey, in which we lay ourselves open to the hard work of transformation.

What do you feel when Jesus says to you, "Do you want to be made well?"

If you can't say yes right now, what would help you to do so? What signs has God given you that show he is trustworthy and works things out your good?

What would "being well" look like for you? What is one step you can take toward being well?

doodles · hopes · fears · lights · prayers · mercies · words · dreams · tears · joys

joys · tears · dreams · words · mercies · prayers · lights · fears · hopes · doodles

determination

Let God In

Take a moment and let God in. Invite him into the places of your heart and your life that you most want to hide from him. Ask him to speak to you about these places and to give you the courage to begin to trust him with your life in ever deeper ways.

Yes, Lord, please come. I invite you into my heart and into my life. I give you permission to walk through the rooms of my heart and the halls of my life. Visit with your healing presence. Come to me here. Come heal me here.

Sit quietly. Rest. Wait. Journal your thoughts, feelings, desires.

_____

_____

_____

_____

_____

_____

_____

_____

_____

_____

_____

Letters from God

Do you realize that I have anointed you and I hold all your hopes in my hands? You are my dearest friend, and I have clothed you with light so that even when there is darkness and you think you cannot see, I know the path you are on. With me you will always be sure. Do not fear. I am with you.

I promise never to leave you alone. I promise to love you for all eternity. I promise to keep you from evil's harm though that does not necessarily mean you will escape all suffering. My sign will never leave your forehead and all will know you are mine.

CHAPTER 5

"I Just Want to Feel Better"

Spiritual Directions

From my journal:

"Scared. What is it? I've felt so good lately—focus, attention, performance, creativity.... Then like a spaceship hurtling through bombs, problems and projects, I'm breaking up and falling apart. I can't stand still. I can't sit still. I can't pray. I can't do anything. Someone please help me. I don't know what to do. The world is racing by and no one cares. I'm bad. I've lost everything. There is no one to help me. Please, someone, please help me. I'm so tired. So very tired."

Do you have a journal entry that captures one of your lowest moments?

Copy this phrase below: *The Lord is my Shepherd. He takes care of me.*

_____

_____

_____

Moment of Contemplation

Picture yourself at one of your lowest moments. How has someone reached out to you? Or how do you need someone to show you they care? What would it be like not being alone with your pain?

Sit quietly. Rest. Wait. Journal your thoughts, feelings, desires.

Holy Darkness

As the legend goes, *She-who-flies-swiftly* was known by all in the forest for her swift flight, and the magnificent color of her feathers made her the joy of all the animals that watched her fly above the trees. One day she broke her wing, and she found safety underneath a tree. The Creator visited her, picked her up, passed his hand over her wing, and placed her gently back under the tree. *She-who-flies-swiftly* began to sing in her sorrow until her song, which ushered from her broken heart, filled the forest with its hauntingly beautiful melody. *She-who-flies-swiftly* never flew again, but the healing touch of the Creator had given her the miracle of song and a new direction in life. Healing comes in many different ways.

What would you like to say to God?

_____

_____

_____

_____

_____

_____

_____

_____

_____

_____

_____

Personal Pages Between God and You

God says, "I will be gracious to you when you call out, and I will answer you quickly. I will give you the bread you are hungry for and the water you are thirsting for. I will not hide myself from you any longer but with your own eyes you will see me, your Teacher. And you will hear from behind you my voice which will say, 'This is the way; walk in it.' On that day I will heal all your wounds."

(cf. Is 30:19ff.)

Sometimes we grade God's love for us by how we feel about ourselves. When we are depressed we can feel lousy—even if we pray a lot for some kind of miracle. God proves his love for us by his fidelity to us: that no matter how alone, sick, or crazy we feel we are, God still breathes us into life. We might think this to be a cruel love—God should let us die and end it all—but I have found that depression yields most beautiful pearls if we have help to walk through the night. Becoming "better" probably is your code word for becoming as you were before your depression. Instead, God dreams something more for you.

Do you know of someone who has developed new qualities of character after an illness? What are some qualities you desire to develop in yourself?

What is a new path God may be pointing out to you?

doodles · hopes · fears · lights · prayers · mercies · words · dreams · tears · joys

joys · tears · dreams · words · mercies · prayers · lights · fears · hopes · doodles

healing

Let God In

Take a moment and let God in. Invite him into the places of your heart and your life that you most want to hide from him. Ask him to speak to you about these places and to give you the courage to begin to trust him with your life in ever deeper ways.

Yes, Lord, please come. I invite you into my heart and into my life. I give you permission to walk through the rooms of my heart and the halls of my life. Visit with your healing presence. Come to me here. Come heal me here.

Sit quietly. Rest. Wait. Journal your thoughts, feelings, desires.

_____

_____

_____

_____

_____

_____

_____

_____

_____

_____

_____

Letters from God

You are truly drawn into my mysteries by the cross. However, I want you to be silent. Do nothing but be present to a flower, a brook, a forest, a mountain range, a sunset. More and more you will find yourself drawn toward me in my mysteries because I am the source of the smallest mystery.

This dark meditation is the theology of which my friends speak. I tell them secrets and give them a radiant light in the depths of their souls. I am calling you to this, and I want you to understand that this journey through darkness is the safest kind of journey. It is openness to me, and I love you.

doodles · hopes · fears · lights · prayers · mercies · words · dreams · tears · joys

joys · tears · dreams · words · mercies · prayers · lights · fears · hopes · doodles

CHAPTER 6

"I Can't Stop Crying"

Spiritual Directions

I picked up the phone and heard my friend weeping. "I don't know what to do," he exclaimed.

"What's wrong," I asked, alarmed and fearing the worst. "Tell me what happened!"

After a muffled sob, he began, "My wife just found out she has cancer and less than six months to live. What am I going to do? What will my kids do without their mother? I don't know what to do. What am I going to do?"

Can you write about an event that sent you on a downward plunge of desperation?

Copy this phrase below: *Even though I walk through the dark valley, I fear no evil, with the Lord at my side.*

_____

_____

_____

Moment of Contemplation

Can you remember a desperate situation that has now passed? What contributed to your being able to move on? How did you feel when you realized the situation was behind you?

Sit quietly. Rest. Wait. Journal your thoughts, feelings, desires.

Holy Darkness

Blessed Charles de Foucauld (1858–1916), once a reckless adventurer, found his heart's desire in a simple life of presence among the Muslim people in the Sahara Desert. He wrote in a meditation on Psalm 2, "It seems as though there is a great abyss between us, and that you look on us with severity. We wonder where we are and where we are going, and it seems as though we are sinking in quicksand, unable to free ourselves. But, my God, you are so good! You call to us, 'Find yourself in me,' and you throw us a solid anchor."[7]

God knows you just as you are, with your history, your fears, your needs, and your tears. God loves you just as you are. God is the one who loves you most, with your garbage, your limitations, and your problems, as well as the beauty you may not be able to see at this time. God is walking toward you, arms outstretched, to help you find meaning in everything. What is most needed is to let God impress you with his love. Even if you feel nothing when you read about God's love for you, say to God, "I believe, even though I cannot see." One day you will no longer need to believe, because you will see. I promise!

What would you like to say to God?

_____

_____

_____

_____

_____

_____

Personal Pages Between God and You

This is heroism—

"To love another when you get nothing in return."

(cf. Lk 6:35)

A few weeks after speaking with my friend whose wife had been diagnosed with cancer, we reconnected. He told me, "I take it a day at a time now. At first I was grasping at every novena I could find to make God heal her. Now, instead, I wake up each morning with a prayer to live with integrity, to respect the dignity of others, and to love her and my children just for that day. All I have is each day to love my wife. I love her so much. Somehow God will see us through whatever happens."

What would heroism look like to you?

What is one step you could take to live heroically? What support will you need? Who will you ask to support you? When and how?

doodles · hopes · fears · lights · prayers · mercies · words · dreams · tears · joys

joys · tears · dreams · words · mercies · prayers · lights · fears · hopes · doodles

doodles · hopes · fears · lights · prayers · mercies · words · dreams · tears · joys

joys · tears · dreams · words · mercies · prayers · lights · fears · hopes · doodles

heroism

Let God In

Take a moment and let God in. Invite him into the places of your heart and your life that you most want to hide from him. Ask him to speak to you about these places and to give you the courage to begin to trust him with your life in ever deeper ways.

Yes, Lord, please come. I invite you into my heart and into my life. I give you permission to walk through the rooms of my heart and the halls of my life. Visit with your healing presence. Come to me here. Come heal me here.

Sit quietly. Rest. Wait. Journal your thoughts, feelings, desires.

_____

_____

_____

_____

_____

_____

_____

_____

_____

_____

_____

_____

_____

How many tears does a heart that has been pierced shed? Can you count them? I will renew in your life the event of my resurrection, even though you may see only Calvary through your tears. In every tear, you reflect my own sorrow, an anguish at your pain, a promise to be with you through the fire, the absolute guarantee that no matter the crookedness of the events of your life, I will bring order, goodness, and beauty in ways that you cannot anticipate. Give up absolute control over what you think is best and let me care for you.

doodles · hopes · fears · lights · prayers · mercies · words · dreams · tears · joys

joys · tears · dreams · words · mercies · prayers · lights · fears · hopes · doodles

CHAPTER 7

"I'm Going Crazy!"

Spiritual Directions

My good friend, the superior of a small community of religious sisters, felt as though she were in a black hole of depression. She was sinking fast and had no idea how to get out. One day she went outside and said aloud, "God, I want out. I've done my part. Now it's up to you." She said she heard a clear voice in her head saying, "Go over to the fence." She did and then noticed a tangled fishing hook and line. She reached up to untangle it. Then she heard these words, "I've already caught you." It was the most direct message from God she had ever received. "Things around me didn't change," she said, "but I began to change. I knew that somehow God had hold of me and was going to see me through."

Can you write about a time when a voice, either God's or another's, put everything you were experiencing into a new light?

Copy this phrase below: *I am held in the palm of God's hand.*

_____

_____

Moment of Contemplation

Do you have a favorite verse from Scripture, or a line of poetry, or a song that has gotten you through a hard time? What happens to you when you return to that powerful passage, recite that poem, or hear that song?

Sit quietly. Rest. Wait. Journal your thoughts, feelings, desires.

_____

_____

_____

_____

_____

_____

_____

_____

_____

_____

_____

_____

_____

_____

Holy Darkness

Stormy passages mark many points in our life. St. Augustine, who documented the complicated story of his own inner conflicts and struggle with grace, put into words for all of us the encounter with God, who, in a single instant, calms our inner seas:

> You called, shouted, broke through my deafness;
> you flared, blazed, banished my blindness;
> you lavished your fragrance, I gasped, and now I pant for you;
> I tasted you, and I hunger and thirst;
> you touched me, and I burned for your peace.[8]

What would you like to say to God?

Humming on the Journey

Personal Pages Between God and You

I've seen their sufferings and I've come to save them.

(cf. Ex 3:7–8)

God is saying your name right now. God is interested in the circumstances of your life. God does not just want to save you, God *is* saving you right now. God liberated the chosen people, but only with their help. They had to trust that this voice was truly God's. They had to make the break from the land of Egypt. They had to walk into the desert. They had to believe that God would provide for them because he loved them.

What do you want to know from God? Is there something you can't quite trust God with?

Can you identify some event that could be the intervention of God in your life?

What is one thing God may be inviting you to do?

caught

Let God In

Take a moment and let God in. Invite him into the places of your heart and your life that you most want to hide from him. Ask him to speak to you about these places and to give you the courage to begin to trust him with your life in ever deeper ways.

Yes, Lord, please come. I invite you into my heart and into my life. I give you permission to walk through the rooms of my heart and the halls of my life. Visit with your healing presence. Come to me here. Come heal me here.

Sit quietly. Rest. Wait. Journal your thoughts, feelings, desires.

_____

_____

_____

_____

_____

_____

_____

_____

_____

_____

_____

_____

Come, I know you are ready to throw in the towel, but it is precisely at this moment that I offer you the leap of faith. You feel me to be far away. Instead, I am right at the door knocking, promising you freedom. Freedom doesn't mean liberation from responsibility—a type of second childhood. No. I offer you a strong freedom—freedom from yourself, if you are willing to walk forward in abandonment to my designs for your life. No life can be compared to another, because infinite are my dreams for my children. I will extract you from wherever you feel caught in. You will experience my power to save as soon as you place your life into my hands. First you must believe, then you will see. Mine are strong hands, but they are safe hands.

doodles · hopes · fears · lights · prayers · mercies · words · dreams · tears · joys

joys · tears · dreams · words · mercies · prayers · lights · fears · hopes · doodles

CHAPTER 8

Start Humming in the Darkness

Spiritual Directions

The waiting room at the behavioral neurology unit was full as I took a seat. I looked around at the people who, like me, visit here frequently for the ongoing treatment of a wide variety of neurological disorders. Once I believed I would get my illness behind me. Now I realize it's about the process, the relationships I forge on the way, the adjustment of my medications, the things I learn about myself and others, the setbacks and triumphs. I live somewhere between the soft dusk and early morning light, which never quite makes it to broad daylight. But if I waited for the noonday victory to begin living, I would never experience any joy. I must start humming now, day by day, in the darkness as it alternates with the dawning light.

What was your initial vision of health? How has it changed?

Copy this phrase below: *Awake my soul. I will awake the dawn.*

_____

_____

Moment of Contemplation

What would help you to be more at peace with yourself right now? Are you self-critical? Ashamed? Angry with yourself? Frustrated? What would help you to be able to live each moment with a bit of hope?

Sit quietly. Rest. Wait. Journal your thoughts, feelings, desires.

Holy Darkness

Even saints who suffered with depression had trouble praying and believing God cared about them or that they were any good. St. Gregory Nazianzus once wrote:

> The breath of life, O Lord, seems spent.
> My body is tense, my mind filled with anxiety,
> yet I have no zest, no energy....
> Dark thoughts constantly invade my head....
> Lord, raise up my soul, revive my body.[9]

In the early 1800s, John Vianney, the Curé of Ars, was the holy pastor of a tiny village in France. Streams of pilgrims made their way to Ars for confession and spiritual advice. Despite his holiness, Vianney felt God to be so far from him that he was afraid he had lost his faith. Vianney feared he was ruining everything and had become an obstacle to God's grace. There was not a moment when he felt that God was satisfied with him. His soul was filled with a deep and profound sadness. When depression seemed to overpower him completely, he would throw himself down before God like "a dog at the feet of his master," and weather the storm with a persevering resolution to love and serve God if he could.

What would you like to say to God?

_____

_____

_____

_____

_____

_____

Personal Pages Between God and You

The LORD helps me, so I am not in disgrace.
The one who vindicates me is near.

(cf. Is 50:7–8)

The Lord is near you, standing by your side, walking with you through the fire and treading the ocean deep. A man whose wife had filed for divorce once said to me, "I prayed every day. If God could raise up armies, why couldn't he save my marriage?" The Scripture verse above is from the third Servant Song of the Prophet Isaiah. The Servant Songs have been seen as a prophecy of Jesus in his passion. Even Jesus himself prayed that the cup of suffering would pass him by, and it seemed God didn't answer. Though he cried out in pain through his passion, Jesus had already decided to pour out on humanity the Father's love in whatever form that would take. The soldier's hands, the driving of the nails, the mockery of the crowd...in the midst of all of this, Jesus followed the Father's desire to embody his love for humanity: to forgive, not to retaliate, to love, not to hate. He commended his spirit into his Father's hands, though he felt the Father to be so far away from him.

When you pray, do you feel God's presence, or do you feel alone?

Can you remember a time when you felt God's presence in your life? What was that like?

doodles · hopes · fears · lights · prayers · mercies · words · dreams · tears · joys

joys · tears · dreams · words · mercies · prayers · lights · fears · hopes · doodles

love

Let God In

Take a moment and let God in. Invite him into the places of your heart and your life that you most want to hide from him. Ask him to speak to you about these places and to give you the courage to begin to trust him with your life in ever deeper ways.

Yes, Lord, please come. I invite you into my heart and into my life. I give you permission to walk through the rooms of my heart and the halls of my life. Visit with your healing presence. Come to me here. Come heal me here.

Sit quietly. Rest. Wait. Journal your thoughts, feelings, desires.

_____

_____

_____

_____

_____

_____

_____

_____

_____

_____

_____

_____

The night seems so long for you now. The cross weighs so heavy. Events seem unexplainable. I feel so far away. Come, tell me what it is like. Share with me your loneliness, your anger, your sense of betrayal, your fatigue. If I say I know what it is like, it might make things worse, but I shared your life on earth so that I could say, "I know. I've been there. My heart is breaking for you." I am standing by your side because I know that you and I can pour love and light into the darkness. Even if you can't believe, desire it to be so, desire to be able to give yourself over to this working of love in the midst of your crosses and darkness. You are meant for bigger things. You have an impact on the world. I am already at work in your heart to give you the strength to love, for love is stronger than every evil and every pain. You will find the cross everywhere—it is the watermark printed in all of creation. It is a beautiful watermark because it is the absolute guarantee of my love for creation. When your love mingles with my love, nothing can stop what will be achieved.

doodles · hopes · fears · lights · prayers · mercies · words · dreams · tears · joys

joys · tears · dreams · words · mercies · prayers · lights · fears · hopes · doodles

CHAPTER 9

"Don't Look the Other Way"

Spiritual Directions

Marlene sat beside her husband. The love and gentle familiarity between the two was touching. "I'm Marlene," she said, "and this is my husband. He's here to be my support." She continued very slowly, "I have been seriously depressed for three years. The doctors can't seem to find a medicine that works for me. I've had eighteen ECT treatments, which have helped somewhat. I guess my question is why? There seems to be no explanation for this depression—I don't have a traumatic past, I wasn't ill. It just came out of the blue and it won't go away." She turned to her husband and he took her hand in his own.

What would you hope to find in a support person?

Copy this phrase below: *I am not afraid for God is with me.*

_____

_____

_____

Moment of Contemplation

Picture a scene—in a movie or in your life—in which you witnessed a person caring deeply for someone in need. How did that move you? What qualities of the person were most attractive to you?

Sit quietly. Rest. Wait. Journal your thoughts, feelings, desires.

_____

_____

_____

_____

_____

_____

_____

_____

_____

_____

_____

_____

_____

_____

_____

Holy Darkness

Henri Nouwen reflected on compassion in his book, *Never Forget.* He said that to have compassion is to suffer with another, to walk into their places of darkest pain. It means to stay with them and not to accept easy excuses to move on or to make one's care depend on another's improvement.

The basic desire to withdraw, the feeling of anger or confusion, the shame that accompanies depression do not normally lend themselves to strong friendships. I am always moved by the kindness of others to me, especially when I am not able to return that kindness. Little by little, I learn from the magnanimity and selflessness of others how to be truly sensitive and self-giving to others. Friendship with a person suffering from depression tests the goodness of both the person themselves and their friends.

What would you like to say to God?

_____

_____

_____

_____

_____

_____

_____

_____

_____

Humming on the Journey

Personal Pages Between God and You

Some play at friendship, but true friends are closer than family.

(cf. Prv 18:24)

Our friendships evolve when we suffer from depression or any other mood disorder. Some friends don't know how to relate to us any longer, others don't have the time or energy to invest in such a relationship. Some would like to show us compassion and give a helping hand, but they don't know how.

What kind of a team do you need to support you? Is there someone you can ask to be a help in one particular area of your life?

How could you ask for support?

What could you do for them in gratitude?

shelter

Let God In

Take a moment and let God in. Invite him into the places of your heart and your life that you most want to hide from him. Ask him to speak to you about these places and to give you the courage to begin to trust him with your life in ever deeper ways.

Yes, Lord, please come. I invite you into my heart and into my life. I give you permission to walk through the rooms of my heart and the halls of my life. Visit with your healing presence. Come to me here. Come heal me here.

Sit quietly. Rest. Wait. Journal your thoughts, feelings, desires.

_____

_____

_____

_____

_____

_____

_____

_____

_____

_____

_____

_____

Letters from God

My child, does it seem that you are not understood? Here is real darkness. No one is near you to catch you when you fall. I am with you *in* the people who have done you kindnesses and tried to reach out to you. Though you may sorrow that specific people are not there to support you, I am placing people all along the way to be my hands, my eyes, my lips. Keep looking and you will see them.

doodles · hopes · fears · lights · prayers · mercies · words · dreams · tears · joys

joys · tears · dreams · words · mercies · prayers · lights · fears · hopes · doodles

CHAPTER 10

Healings Are Not "Success Stories"

Spiritual Directions

Every time I return to Ohio, two wonderful people make sure to stop by and give me a hug. Husband and wife, they have had a rocky marriage. The family had suffered from his alcoholism and depression, the children left home when they came of age, never to return. She had stayed faithful to him, doing her utmost to provide the best for her children. Now they are very giving, spiritual people, living a gentle and sober life. Neither of them have seen their grandchildren, because their children will not accept the possibility of any change in their father's behavior. This couple carries this pain within them always, adopting people in need as members of their family.

What open wounds remain in your heart despite your journey of healing?

Copy this phrase below: *Depression and despair do not have the last word, not now, not ever.*

_____

_____

Moment of Contemplation

Gather together the indications you have that God has been active in your life since you began to use this journal. Where has there been progress? Who celebrates that progress? How do *you* celebrate that progress? Who cannot see it, and keeps you locked in a label?

Sit quietly. Rest. Wait. Journal your thoughts, feelings, desires.

Holy Darkness

The sufferings that people embrace with God often take on some of God's immensity and mystery. Benedict Joseph Labré made the world his cloister when people repeatedly told him he did not have a religious vocation. His life's dream was dashed, but he began a slow, life-long pilgrimage marked by scrupulosity and mystical prayer, ridicule and acts of charity. Only just before his death did he become free of scruples and depression. Like Benedict, you may know only the anguished struggle. You may feel useless in comparison to your former abilities. It does not matter. Christ creates a sculpture of your life, using the illnesses of your body and the sufferings of your mind to chisel the richest details. While depression may affect your dreams and lifestyle, the intensity of your spirit's yearning transforms darkness into life within you.

What would you like to say to God?

_____

_____

_____

_____

_____

_____

_____

_____

_____

_____

Humming on the Journey

Personal Pages Between God and You

Your self is hidden with Christ in God.

(cf. Col 3:3)

For most of us depression is an ongoing illness, showing up in different ways: anxiety, confused thinking, exhaustion, anger, listlessness.... How does one live with this intruder upsetting life when least expected? Routines and rhythms can lull us into feeling that things are in control, the worst is over, smooth sailing lies ahead. Then it reappears, taking on some previously unexperienced form.

Our thoughts and feelings are, according to Martin Laird, a patchwork quilt making up our personality.[10] What we are able to comprehend about ourselves, however, is not our deepest reality. Beyond our thinking and feeling there is grace, there is the inseparable unity between God and ourselves that makes us—and remakes us—good. The grace of salvation, our hiddenness with Christ in God, does not depend on our emotional stability. Our rambling thoughts and emotions deceive us, generating the illusion that we are separate and separated from God. But as the Flemish mystic John Ruysbroeck states, the Lord enters the marrow of our bones, consuming us. He swoops down on us to take over our entire life so that he may change it into his.[11] Beyond our thoughts, God's activity within and for us powerfully transforms us.

When have you experienced the ground of your being beyond your thinking and feeling? Perhaps it was watching a sunset, or seeing your newborn child, or sitting by the ocean?

What could you do to make these grounding moments more a part of your life? What rhythms of prayer do you want to instate as you move forward in life?

96

doodles · hopes · fears · lights · prayers · mercies · words · dreams · tears · joys

joys · tears · dreams · words · mercies · prayers · lights · fears · hopes · doodles

doodles · hopes · fears · lights · prayers · mercies · words · dreams · tears · joys

joys · tears · dreams · words · mercies · prayers · lights · fears · hopes · doodles

illumination

Let God In

Take a moment and let God in. Invite him into the places of your heart and your life that you most want to hide from him. Ask him to speak to you about these places and to give you the courage to begin to trust him with your life in ever deeper ways.

Yes, Lord, please come. I invite you into my heart and into my life. I give you permission to walk through the rooms of my heart and the halls of my life. Visit with your healing presence. Come to me here. Come heal me here.

Sit quietly. Rest. Wait. Journal your thoughts, feelings, desires.

_____

_____

_____

_____

_____

_____

_____

_____

_____

_____

_____

_____

_____

Be gentle with yourself. Your responsibilities may be many, your workload heavy, family matters may weigh on you, but be gentle with yourself. Give all your cares to me and I will care for you. Seek first my kingdom—my peace and patience, my meekness and poverty—and all else will be given you besides.

I am holding you in my hand, protecting you from the cruelties you could sometimes meet. I understand what it means to suffer and to survive depression. I know it is a daily struggle and a moment-by-moment survival. I am here so that you can start again each day and each moment. You can trust that, okay?

doodles · hopes · fears · lights · prayers · mercies · words · dreams · tears · joys

joys · tears · dreams · words · mercies · prayers · lights · fears · hopes · doodles

Appendix

Some Symptoms of Depression

- Crying
- Anger
- Weight loss or gain
- Fear and anxiety
- Violent mood swings
- Withdrawal
- Irritability
- Hopelessness
- Feelings of guilt
- Oversensitivity
- Bursting into tears
- Feelings of inadequacy
- Change of sleep patterns
- Uncontrollable feelings of despair
- No interest in food, or unusual overeating
- Apathy
- Feeling worthless
- Lacking all motivation
- Sense of futility

Suggestions for Support

Not all these are helpful or possible for everyone all the time. Choose those best suited for you at this time.

- Talk with a good friend.
- Reach out to help someone.
- Go to a support group.
- Do a hobby with someone.
- Arrange to be around others.
- Spend time with a pet.
- Go to Mass with a friend.
- Go for a walk with someone.
- Call a crisis clinic or hotline.
- Exercise with someone.
- Join a parish committee with a friend.
- Chat with a family member.
- Spend time with good friends.
- Let yourself be held by someone you love.
- Talk with someone in your parish.
- Pray.
- Choose to be around people who don't criticize, judge, or want to change you, but who accept you for who you are at this point in your life.
- Be okay with who you are, not trying to live up to another's expectations.

Basics for Surviving Depression

- Get eight good hours of sleep each night. Don't stay in bed longer or cut your sleep shorter.
- Take a walk—even a short one—between 11:00 A.M. and 2:00 P.M. The bright light has an antidepressant effect. The exercise gives you more energy.

- Abstain from the use of alcohol and street drugs, both of which induce depression and prevent antidepressants from working effectively.
- Eat a well-balanced diet.
- Create a schedule for yourself.
- Take medication as prescribed.
- Avoid the use of products that contain aspartame (for example, Equal or NutraSweet). Studies have shown that these products can increase a person's depression if he or she is already depressed.
- Get a bird or another easy-to-care-for pet. This provides company and can also be a conversation starter when talking with friends.
- Choose a friend that you can check in with every day. A depressed person can find it difficult to get out of a rut or a destructive pattern of thinking. Even a phone conversation lasting just a few minutes can be sufficient to help you see a different perspective. A consistent phone call "appointment" can interrupt the "forever" feeling of depression.
- Daily exercise, even as simple as a brisk walk, will give you more energy.
- Keep a journal.

Breath Prayers

Short prayers can be said in rhythm with your breathing during the day to keep yourself aware of God's presence. We often think God is far from us, but in reality God can never be absent from us. It is our thoughts that create the illusion of separation. Short prayers that we "breathe" to God during the day, whenever our mind is idle, can strengthen our awareness of God's loving presence to us. You can also use any line from Scripture, especially the Psalms.

Jesus.

Jesus, mercy.

Jesus, I trust in you.

I am the apple of your eye.

I am waiting for you. Lord, you are coming.

Lord Jesus Christ, have mercy on me.

I am with you, Lord. You are with me.

A Prayer to Jesus, My Inmost Counselor [12]

Human counselors have remarkable gifts of listening and offering insight. Yet, these persons cannot see our thoughts, nor probe our inmost heart. Only Jesus is the ultimate counselor and Divine Healer.

Lord, the psalmist says, "You have searched me and known me...you discern my thoughts from far away...and are acquainted with all my ways" (Ps 139:1–3). Even though you already know all about me, I need to tell you what is bothering me, Lord. My thoughts are racing, confused, angry, and anxious. I need to talk to someone, and you are always available. Please listen, Lord. Correct my wayward thoughts. You are the Truth. Let me think rationally, calmly, without worry.

Banish every thought of self-hatred, despair, or panic that intrudes on my peace.

At times I feel trapped by my fears and anxiety. Release me from these bonds, dear Lord.

You said, "Come apart with me" (see Mt 11:28; Mk 6:31). In prayer, I want to distance myself from all that makes me anxious and lay it aside for you to handle. I want to sit at your feet, "to be still and know that you are God" (see Ps 46:10). I want to be confident that you can answer my prayer.

Lord, many things make me angry. This spills into my prayer and spoils my outlook on life. Give me an uplifting life-perspective, imbedded in your Gospel teaching. I know that alone I cannot quiet my anger. Direct me to practical means and, if needed, therapy and medicine, which can help me manage my emotions. Lord, in the Gospel, a man was gashing himself and was so tormented that he lived among the tombs (see Mk 5:1–13). At times I feel entombed by this illness. Lay your healing hand on my head. Give me peace and anchor me in the firm conviction that you love me more than I can ever love myself. Thank you for this love and for listening to me. Amen.

Notes

1. Excerpt from *Given to God: Daily Readings with Evelyn Underhill* by Delroy Oberg, p. 163. Copyright © 1992 by Dartman, Longman and Todd, 1 Spen-cer Court, 140–142 Wandsworth High Street, London SW18 4JJ, England. Used with permission of Dartman, Longman and Todd.

2. Excerpt from *Essential Writings* by Chiara Lubich, p. 132. Copyright © 2007 by New City Press, Inc., Hyde Park, New York 12538. Used with permission of New City Press.

3. Cf. Richard Payne, ed., *George Herbert, The Country Parson, The Temple* (New York: Paulist Press, 1981), p. 291.

4. Poem by Bernadette M. Reiss, FSP, March 15, 2007. Used with permission.

5. Cf. Lucy Beckett, *In the Light of Christ* (San Francisco: Ignatius, 2006), p. 288.

6. Cf. T. S. Eliot, *The Complete Poems and Plays* (New York: Harcourt and Brace, 1962), pp. 295–387.

7. Excerpt from *Charles de Foucauld: Journey of the Spirit* by Cathy Wright, lsj, p. 70. Copyright © 2005, Pauline Books & Media, 50 St. Paul's Ave., Boston, MA 02130.

8. Excerpt from *Confessions* by St. Augustine, copyright © 1997 by New City Press, Inc. Used with permission of Augustinian Heritage Institute.

9. Excerpt from *Surviving Depression: A Catholic Approach by* Kathryn J. Hermes, FSP, p. 109. Copyright © 2003, Pauline Books & Media.

10. Cf. Martin Laird, *Into the Silent Land* (New York: Oxford University Press, 2006), p. 14.

11. Ibid., p. 15.

12. Excerpt from *Tender Mercies* by Mary Peter Martin, FSP, pp. 13–14. Copyright © 2007, Pauline Books & Media.

BOOKS & MEDIA

The Daughters of St. Paul operate book and media centers at the following addresses. Visit, call, or write the one nearest you today, or find us on the World Wide Web, www.pauline.org

CALIFORNIA
3908 Sepulveda Blvd, Culver City, CA 90230   310-397-8676
2460 Broadway Street, Redwood City, CA 94063   650-369-4230
5945 Balboa Avenue, San Diego, CA 92111   858-565-9181

FLORIDA
145 S.W. 107th Avenue, Miami, FL 33174   305-559-6715

HAWAII
1143 Bishop Street, Honolulu, HI 96813   808-521-2731
Neighbor Islands call: 866-521-2731

ILLINOIS
172 North Michigan Avenue, Chicago, IL 60601   312-346-4228

LOUISIANA
4403 Veterans Memorial Blvd, Metairie, LA 70006   504-887-7631

MASSACHUSETTS
885 Providence Hwy, Dedham, MA 02026   781-326-5385

MISSOURI
9804 Watson Road, St. Louis, MO 63126   314-965-3512

NEW JERSEY
561 U.S. Route 1, Wick Plaza, Edison, NJ 08817   732-572-1200

NEW YORK
150 East 52nd Street, New York, NY 10022   212-754-1110

PENNSYLVANIA
9171-A Roosevelt Blvd, Philadelphia, PA 19114   215-676-9494

SOUTH CAROLINA
243 King Street, Charleston, SC 29401   843-577-0175

TENNESSEE
4811 Poplar Avenue, Memphis, TN 38117   901-761-2987

TEXAS
114 Main Plaza, San Antonio, TX 78205   210-224-8101

VIRGINIA
1025 King Street, Alexandria, VA 22314   703-549-3806

CANADA
3022 Dufferin Street, Toronto, ON M6B 3T5   416-781-9131

¡También somos su fuente para libros, DVDs,
y música en español!